Describing Words

Adjectives, Adverbs, and Prepositions

Anita Ganeri

www.raintreepublishers.co.uk
Visit our website to find out
more information about
Raintree books.

To order:
☎ Phone 0845 6044371
📄 Fax +44 (0) 1865 312263
✉ Email myorders@raintreepublishers.co.uk

Customers from outside the UK please telephone +44 1865 312262

Raintree is an imprint of Capstone Global Library Limited,
a company incorporated in England and Wales having its
registered office at 7 Pilgrim Street, London, EC4V 6LB
– Registered company number: 6695582

Text © Capstone Global Library Limited 2012
First published in hardback in 2012
First published in paperback in 2013
The moral rights of the proprietor have been asserted.

Edited by Daniel Nunn, Rebecca Rissman, and Sian Smith
Designed by Joanna Hinton-Malivoire
Picture research by Tracy Cummins
Original illustrations © Capstone Global Library
Illustrated by Joanna Hinton-Malivoire
Production by Eirian Griffiths
Originated by Capstone Global Library Ltd
Printed in China

ISBN 978 1 406 23238 7 (hardback)
15 14 13 12 11
10 9 8 7 6 5 4 3 2 1

ISBN 978 1 406 23245 5 (paperback)
16 15 14 13 12
10 9 8 7 6 5 4 3 2 1

British Library Cataloguing in Publication Data
Ganeri, Anita, 1961-
Describing words: adjectives, adverbs, and prepositions.
(Getting to grips with grammar)
 425-dc22
A full catalogue record for this book is available from the
British Library.

Acknowledgements
We would like to thank the following for permission to reproduce
photographs and artworks: Dreamstime.com p.16 © (Viorel
Sima); Shutterstock pp.5 (© AnetaPics), 7 (© Cory Thoman), 8 (©
Tony Oshlick), 9 (© Kirill Vorobyev), 11 (© Susan McKenzie), 12 (Eric
Isselée), 13 (© Johan Swanepoel), 17 (© sunsetman), 18 (© David
Sales Batista), 19 (© Don Purcell), 21 (© Brocreative), 23 (© Supri
Suharjoto), 24 (© DM7), 26 (© majeczka), 27 (© infografick), 28 (©
Laurie Barr), 29 (© anyaivanova), 30 (© Maxim Slugin).

Every effort has been made to contact copyright holders
of material reproduced in this book. Any omissions will
be rectified in subsequent printings if notice is given to the
publisher.

Contents

Some words are shown in bold, **like this**.
You can find them in the glossary on page 31.

What is grammar?

Grammar is a set of rules that helps you to write and speak a language. Grammar is important because it helps people to understand each other.

brown runs dog very My fast.

Without grammar, this **sentence** doesn't make sense.

In grammar, words are divided into different types. These are called parts of speech. They show how words are used. This book is about parts of speech called **adjectives**, **adverbs**, and **prepositions**.

My brown dog runs very fast.

Grammar turns the jumbled-up words into a sentence.

What is an adjective?

An **adjective** is a word that describes things. It tells you more about a **noun** or a **pronoun** (a naming word).

Today, the weather is sunny and warm.

'Sunny' and 'warm' are adjectives. They describe the 'weather', which is a noun.

'Huge', 'orange', and 'hairy' are adjectives. They describe the 'monster', which is a noun.

The monster was huge, orange, and hairy.

It is easy to spot an adjective. If a word tells you what a noun or pronoun is like, it is an adjective.

Spot the adjective

Look at this list of words. How many **adjectives** can you spot? Remember that an adjective describes a **noun** or **pronoun** (a naming word).

smelly

jumped

tasty

fierce

funny

dinosaur

'Smelly', 'tasty', 'fierce', and 'funny' are adjectives. 'Jumped' and 'dinosaur' are *not* adjectives.

Look at the three **sentences** below. How many adjectives can you spot? There is one in the first sentence, two in the second sentence, and three in the third sentence.

The elephant is enormous.

I am wearing a long, red dress.

My little cat is stripy and furry.

The adjectives are 'enormous', 'long', 'red', 'little', 'stripy', and 'furry'.

More adjectives

Adjectives can describe **nouns** and **pronouns** in other ways, too. Some adjectives ask questions. They are words like 'which', 'what', and 'whose'. Some adjectives point things out. They are words like 'that', 'these', and 'those'.

Which hat do you like best?

Those children are hungry.

'Which' is an adjective that asks a question. 'Those' is an adjective that points the children out.

Your shoes are very dirty.

I want some cake.

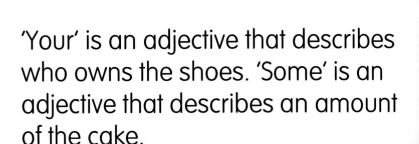

'Your' is an adjective that describes who owns the shoes. 'Some' is an adjective that describes an amount of the cake.

Some adjectives describe who owns something. They are words like 'my', 'our', and 'your'. Some adjectives show the amount of something. They are words like 'some', 'many', and 'all'.

Comparing words

You can also use **adjectives** to compare different people or things. To compare two people or things, you usually add 'er' to an ordinary adjective. This makes a **comparative** adjective.

That giraffe is tall.

It is taller than this zebra.

'Tall' is an ordinary adjective. 'Taller' is a comparative adjective.

To compare three or more people or things, you usually add 'est' to an ordinary adjective. This makes a **superlative** adjective.

This giraffe is taller than the other one.

This giraffe is the tallest of them all.

'Taller' is a comparative adjective.
'Tallest' is a superlative adjective.

More comparing words

Some **adjectives** make their **comparatives** and **superlatives** in a different way. If adding 'er' or 'est' is awkward, you put 'more' or 'most' in front of the word instead.

Roses are more beautiful than daffodils.

Tulips are the most beautiful flowers.

'More beautiful' is a comparative adjective. 'Most beautiful' is a superlative adjective.

Adjective	Comparative	Superlative
good	better	best
bad	worse	worst
many	more	most
little	less	least

Can you think of any other examples to add to the list?

Some adjectives do not follow any rules. You can see some of them in the table above. You just have to learn their comparatives and superlatives.

What is an adverb?

An **adverb** is another type of describing word. It is a word that tells you more about a **verb** (a doing word).

'Noisily' is an adverb. It describes how the dog barked.

The dog barked noisily.

It is easy to find out if something is an adverb. Adverbs tell you how, where, when, or why something happens.

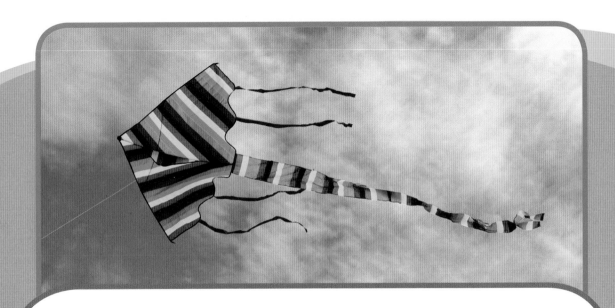

I flew my new kite outside.

'Outside' is an adverb. It describes where you flew your kite.

Spot the adverb

Look at this list of words. How many **adverbs** can you spot? Remember that an adverb is a word that describes a **verb** (an action or doing word).

angrily

merrily

soon

yesterday

witch

fierce

'Angrily', 'merrily', 'yesterday', and 'soon' are adverbs. 'Witch' and 'fierce' are *not* adverbs.

Look at the three **sentences** below. Can you find the adverbs? There is one in the first sentence, two in the second, and three in the third.

She ate her lunch quickly.

I sang the song softly and well.

The owl hooted suddenly and loudly, then quietly.

The adverbs are 'quickly', 'softly', 'well', 'suddenly', 'loudly', and 'quietly'.

Making adverbs

Many **adverbs** end in 'ly'. You make them by adding 'ly' to an **adjective**.

Adjective	Adverb
clever	cleverly
quick	quickly
soft	softly
slow	slowly

Can you think of any other 'ly' adverbs?

The baby has a happy face.

The baby smiles happily.

'Happy' is an adjective. To turn it into an adverb, take off the 'y' and add 'ily' to the end.

If an adjective ends in 'y', you change the 'y' into 'i' before adding 'ly'. You can see how this works above.

More adverbs

Some **adverbs** do not end in 'ly'. These are often adverbs that describe when something happens. Other adverbs describe how often something happens or where something happens.

First **I washed my face.**

I never **eat tomatoes.**

My guinea pig sleeps here.

'First' is an adverb that describes when something happens. 'Never' is an adverb that describes how often something happens. 'Here' is an adverb that describes where something happens.

Some **adjectives** change completely when they become adverbs.

'Good' is an adjective.
Its adverb form is 'well'.

He is a good dancer.

He can dance very well.

Adjective or adverb?

Some **adjectives** also end in 'ly'. It is easy to get them mixed up with **adverbs**.

'Friendly' is an adjective. To turn it into an adverb, you have to use the **phrase** 'in a friendly way' instead of a word.

The dragon was friendly.

It grinned in a friendly way.

This homework is very hard.

I work hard every day.

The first 'hard' is an adjective. It describes 'homework', which is a noun. The second 'hard' is an adverb. It describes 'work', which is a verb.

Some words can be adjectives or adverbs. It depends on their job in a **sentence**. If they describe **nouns** or **pronouns**, they are adjectives. If they describe **verbs**, they are adverbs.

What is a preposition?

A **preposition** is a word that tells you where someone or something is. Prepositions are usually placed before **nouns** or **pronouns**.

'In' is a preposition. It describes where the flowers grow. 'Under' is a preposition. It describes where the cat is.

The flowers grow in the garden.

The cat is under the table.

You also use prepositions to describe when something happens. This can be a time, day, date, or period of time.

After breakfast, I went for a walk.

On my birthday, I will open my presents.

'After' and 'on' are prepositions. They describe when things happened, or when they will happen.

Preposition or adverb?

Some words can be used as **prepositions** or **adverbs**. It is easy to get them mixed up. Remember that a preposition normally has a **noun** or a **pronoun** after it.

The monkey climbed up the tree.

The monkey climbed up.

The first 'up' is a preposition. It is followed by a noun. The second 'up' is an adverb. It tells you about the **verb**.

The train chugged along the track.

The train chugged along.

The first 'along' is a preposition.
It tells you where the train chugs.
The second 'along' is an adverb.
It tells you how the train chugs.

Remember that a preposition also describes the relationship of one thing to another. This can help you to tell which words are prepositions.

Find describing words

Look at the picture below. Which **adjectives**, **adverbs**, and **prepositions** can you think of to describe what is happening?

Possible answers: many; crunchy; high, highest; outside; happily; energetically; on; in; over; through

Glossary

adjective a describing word that tells you more about a noun or a pronoun

adverb a describing word that tells you more about a verb

comparative an adjective that says 'more'

grammar a set of rules that helps you speak or write clearly

noun a naming word

phrase a group of words that does not contain a verb (doing word)

preposition a word that tells you where someone or something is

pronoun a word that stands for a noun

sentence a group of words that makes sense on its own

superlative an adjective that says 'most'

verb a doing or action word

Find out more

Books

Go Further with Grammar, Ruth Thomson (Belitha Press, 2004)

Grammar and Punctuation for School (Homework Helpers), Ladybird (Ladybird Books, 2009)

Grammar Ray series, Andrew Carter (Evans Brothers, 2009)

Websites

www.bbc.co.uk/schools/ks2bitesize/english/spelling_grammar/
Learn about types of words and test yourself on the grammar games.

www.childrensuniversity.manchester.ac.uk/interactives/literacy/ wordclasses/adjectives.asp
Find out more about adjectives and try an adjective game and quiz.

Index